All About Jeffrey Hunter

By: Michelle Bernier

Published by Createspace in 2009

To actor William Shatner—The best starship captain of all! As Mr. Shatner's life story is already in published print I offer the life story of the man 99.9% as good at being the head of the same ship!

Chapter List

Foreword

Jeffrey Hunter. The name that means a lot to both Trekkies (Star Trek fans term) and non-Trekkies alike. This book will look at the biographical life of this very simply fascinating actor and the critical aspects of his film career. We'll discuss his motives in life for very possibly how he became the man he became! And we'll try to find his motives in his actions! Let's now begin with a look at Mr. Hunter!

Chapter One

Jeffrey Hunter's life story

Jeffrey Hunter came into the world in New Orleans, Louisiana on November 25, 1926 (some magazine sources listed his year of birth as 1925). His name at birth was Henry Herbert McKinnies Jr. His dad Henry Sr. was a sale engineer. His mom Edith Lois (Burgess) McKinnies was a housewife. The family was not a showbiz one but it's worth noting they did have a distant relative named Eric Walcott Barnes, who in the 1930's was made Broadway actor of the year! Was knowledge of Barnes a contributing factor to how Jeff became an actor?

Another family fact worth noting is that the family on the father's side was related to former US President Zachary Taylor. Jeff often seemed to have great American patriotism in his films (like when he played a US military man in the 1960 John Ford directed film Seargent Rutledge) and in real life—was this relation to a US president at least a little of the reason?

For the first four years of the future movie star's life the family went on residing in this very famous French-American city. Then thanks to the depression they moved to Milwaukee, Wisconsin and there Jeff (then called Hank) did the remainder of his growing up. Not long after moving to the "beer city" Jeff got appendicitis, periontitis and nephritis. Fortunately he survived all three and very nicely recovered and went to a happy youth.

Some of the schools the boy attended in Milwaukee were the Richards Street Grade School for one. He also attended Christ Episcopal Church where he served as an acolyte attending alter (unintentional training for his film role as Jesus Christ?). One of his childhood friends was a boy named Robert Head. Head much later recollected some of the experiences he remembered having with Jeff. Head claimed the two saw the hit Spencer Tracy film Captains Courageous and after having done so Jeff wanted to see the film again. He went to his own mother and asked if he could see CC. His mother pointed out he'd already seen the film but Jeff begged and went into an impressive reenactment of a scene of the film and, impressed, Edith gave her ok! An actor was blooming!

Jeff had many hobbies as a kid. He put on puppet shows in his backyard and charged neighbors to see them. He was a sketch with disguises. Once at the age of 12 Jeff, in a probably rare misbehaving moment, put on monster makeup and went to lady neighbor's house and frightened her senseless. He even went around to the back of her house and frightened her some her. Her husband then came on the scene and then very, very sternly warned Jeff against doing such mischievous pranks!

Among Jeff's other many hobbies were electric trains and fishing. He did these with his dad (whom, like he was with his mother, he was close to). Jeff said once that he went fishing for over twelve hours with his dad and they didn't catch a bite but Jeff had a great time all the same! Jeff also had dogs. One was a Dachshund named Poochie. The other a Fox Terrier they called Buddy!

Eventually Jeff went on to Whitefish Bay High School. While a student there his hobbies included playing guitar and banjo. No bio on Hunter's life would be complete without mentioning his strong love of football. The nice thoughtful boy played the game from around age 11 on—he had won a statewide contest (held by the paper The Milwaukee Journal) for dropping, passing and place kicking in the juvenile division. Also, it worth noting in high school he would date girls (including one girl a little older than him named Mary Mockley). Jeff was not only a rather excellent athlete (though Edith overprotected him when he played making him wear more protective gear than most players) but a fine student as well. He was president of the sophomore class and in his senior year president of the student body as well.

He also did acting in high school. One of his first bits in stage acting was playing a 60 year old man in a play version of Goldilocks and the Three Bears for the Children's Theater! While later doing another Children's Theater play (as a villain) Jeff also auditioned for the Children's Theater on the Air and got radio parts. Radio would be a big element in Jeff's life for a while to come!

Back to in person acting. A New York summer stock acting troop (called the Port Players) came to Milwaukee and Jeff met up with them. It parlayed into his doing three

Summers worth of acting with the troop. When performing along side them Jeff got his probably first ever acting coverage by a periodical (again the Milwaukee Journal). In a July 18,1943 MJ article on the Port Players the article said that the lad (still called Henry McKinnies) had given a performance par excellent! While, with the Port Players, Jeff played things such as bellboys, sailors and musicians for a while he didn't seem to make any actual money while acting. He did eventually make $12.50 a show when he was in a program called Those Who Serve. This was not with the Port Players but rather in a high school production.

Jeff intended eventually to go on to play college football but he broke his ankle arch and it did in his football future (he had previous football injuries like a broken nose). In 1945 Jeff graduated from high school and headed right into the US Navy still fighting Japan at the time. The Navy took the patriotic lad but refused his request to become a radar man (they already had their quota of them) and instead sent him for primary training. Very soon World War Two ended but Jeff lasted a while longer in the service. He was a radio technician and he was stationed at the Ninth Naval District Headquarters doing teletype work (perhaps this was good unintentional training for when he played military figures on film later). While at the Headquarters Jeff came down with a very bad case of the dreaded measles. As a result of complications from the disease the Navy medically discharged him in 1946!

With his real life military service now behind him Jeff headed to Northwestern University in Chicago! Here he majored in both speech and radio (and minored in the modern science of psychology). During his college life he appeared in NWU productions like Years Ago by Ruth Gordon. He also went with the NWU summer stock company top Eagles Mere, Pennsylvania where he did plays like Payment Deferred and (more notably) Gratiano in William Shakespeare's Merchant of Venice. He was also on the NWU Radio Workshop and Radio Guild. Even more notably perhaps was his with the NBC Radio Institute in Chicago.

In 1949 he appeared in his first film. It was David Bradley's production of Shakespeare's great historical play—Julius Caesar. Shot in Chicago (partially at the city's Museum of Science subbing for ancient Rome) the film had actor-future superstar Charlton Heston in the cast. In a lot of ways Heston's life would parallel Hunter's. Heston had attended NWU in Chicago as well (but before Jeff did). Heston also broke his own nose playing high school football. And both men would make their greatest acting marks playing religious figures (for Heston it would be Moses) and both would be in the start of sci-fi sagas that would go on without them (for Heston it would the first two Planet of the Apes films). Both had a rather serious approach to acting. Both were taught at NWU by acting teacher Alvina Kraus. Both would be on radio and have even more in common (see below).

Once filming on JC wrapped Jeff was now graduated from NWU and he headed off (in a car Henry Sr. purchased for him) to California to enroll in UCLA in the southern part of that western state. His aim: to get a master's degree in radio!

At UCLA Jeff took master's classes to be able to teach radio should he not have been able to be successful on the mike itself. He also did more stage work. He got more stage work as well. He was doing a play called All My Sons. When the play opened Jeff met two talent scouts. At first he thought it was a joke perpetrated by his classmates. But no--- it was for real!!!!!!!!!

One scout was from Paramount and the other 20th Century Fox! They each wanted eyecatching, 6'1 Jeff to come to the their own studio and be tested for a possible film contract. He agreed to visit both studios. At Paramount he screen tested with Ed Begley Sr. But Jeff signed no contract yet. Right after his Fox screen test crafty Fox (!) head Darryl F. Zanuck immediately signed Jeff to a studio contract (Paramount hadn't acted as quick and when they drew up their own contract for him it was too late)

Jeff became a Fox contract player. It was also at this time Jeff stopped being Henry McKinnies to the world. A duo of slightly contradictory accounts of how this exactly happened follows. One source said Jeff's agent at Fox told him McKinnies wouldn't do for a screen name and Jeff wrote some names on cards and came up with hi stage name. Another account seems to suggest Zanuck himself changed the name!

Whatever the case maybe Jeffrey now began his Hollywood film career and he did so by starring with actress Debra Pagent in the film 14 Hours. He played a stock boy who meets a girl while they watch an attempted suicide jumper on the ledge of a building. More Fox work followed for this male youngster. He appeared in Call me Mister as a GI. And he played a college Casanova in the film Take Care of My Little Girl. While he made the latter film his parents came to Hollywood and visited him. When the same premiered later in Milwaukee, Edith told a local newspaper that Jeff's part as a Casanova was nothing like his much nicer real life self.

On the more romantic side of things it was during his very early Hollywood career that Jeff met a beautiful Hollywood film actress named Barbara Rush. They met from mutual friends. Their first date was a beach one but Jeff unromantically spear fished while Barbara watched. This date summed up their personalities—Jeff athletic and Barbara not. (Some of the couple's friends felt that outside of being eye catching and young the two performers had very little in common.)

More romantic dates followed and Jeff proposed to Barbara while the two were on different sets making different films (Jeff was making a film called The Frogman). The couple was married Dec. 1, 1950.

Over the course of the next 16 months Jeff and Barbara were together only for just eight of them. Their busy film schedules kept them away for so long. Jeff did films like Dreamboat with the legendary Ginger Rogers.

Their home (when they were together) was a furnished two-bedroom apartment in Westwood Village. Hunter was already a singing and instrument-playing musician and to please his new wife he added the organ (an instrument she already knew how to play) to his list of instruments he could play himself. He also danced with her a lot in public even though he never was very good at it (more of how little they really had in common!). The two really never argued, they just would at times mutually disagree! Occasionally famous Hollywood friends like Debbie Reynolds, Mitzi Gaynor and Jeff's good mutual friend Robert Wagner (among others) stopped by the apartment for dinner!

Before too long, in 1952, Barbara became pregnant with their first and only child (together)! It was a son Christopher. Just a few days after his birth Jeff had to go the UK to film a movie called Sailor of the King. He said that he was so nervous first learning to hold his child. Despite the busy schedule (Barbara herself stated) Jeff was a very, very dedicated new father. The actor believed in giving his son (in pretty much the former's own words) a solid background and a way that wasn't prejudiced to look at details in life and advantages that made for sound life and fine education along with understanding.

Despite all the healthy attitude Jeff tried to instill into his marriage and fatherhood thanks to all the career time he and his wife spent away from each other the missus wanted a divorce! And in 1955 that is just what happened!

Barbara took the then three year old Christopher with her and Jeff found his new life quite an empty one. Not only was his wife kid largely gone from his life but his career parts dried up for a while too. A tough change of life from the full life he just lead for sure! But remember that Jeff had gone to college minoring in psychology (see above). He was better equipped than most to deal with this. He soon looked on the (actually somewhat) bright side of all this! He knew his boy was very safe and in fine hands with the latter's rather prosperous, very beautiful, intelligent actress-mom raising him. Jeff's time could be his own again. He began to fill his time by reading a great deal and going skin diving a lot too. While Jeff probably longed (very very!) hard for his beautiful ex-wife remember Hollywood had many other voluptuous ladies around! The results were so-so on him emotionally!

Eventually though his career phone started ringing again and parts started to come back. One part he opted for without being offered was of a half-breed Indian in the-to-be John Ford-directed film The Searchers. Jeff was told by Ford this wasn't his type of role. But Jeff met up with Ford again and the former had slicked back his dark hair and displayed a healthy tan (to look more Indian-like). Ford didn't yet give him the part but he told Jeff not to get a haircut until he heard from him (Ford). Jeff felt he some how now had the role and he did get it! The movie also featured western action legend John Wayne as a former Confederate serviceman. Vera Miles played Jeff's love interest. He and Hunter go searching for a missing girl (played by the then teenage Natalie Wood—who'd in real life end up marrying Jeff's and friend sometimes screen co-star Bob Wagner). The Searchers was an almost enormous financial and critical success at the box office in 1956 and became one of Jeff's biggest hits (but more were to follow (see below)).

Jeff soon did another western, far less popular, with his mutual pal Bob Wagner. True story of Jesse James! Nicholas Ray was director!

In 1957 when Jeff was making another film he met a woman on the set. The lady's name was Joan Bartlett. She was doubling for the film's leading lady. For probably the first time since his divorce from Barbara Jeff got involved romantically with a woman. She had a son, Steele, from a previous marriage, the boy being about the same age as Jeff's son Christopher. Despite a budding romance of love when the film production finished the two parted company. Jeff tried to go back to his solitary-but-free lifestyle but he missed the romance of the lady he nicknamed Dusty! Eventually she called Jeff up on the phone to tell him about a modeling job she had been offered! She would be coming to Hollywood to work and Jeff was the only person around there she actually knew. Did he have any advice for her? Jeff offered his advice to her and his love! The two were soon married.

Son after the wedding Jeff and Dusty went to Europe where Jeff was shooting a film. On the way back to America (by ship) they got thirst and they, in haste, drank from a sink that had a "DON'T DRINK THIS WATER" sign on it! They both got sick---especially Jeff he came down with a complete case of hepatitis (this was long before there was any hepatitis vaccine)! He was very 100% helplessly sick for weeks (he had to be spoon fed his meals). Dusty had to tend to him plus her own son and Jeff's son (Barbara was away making a film and left Christopher with Jeff and Dusty). She managed to and when Jeff finally recovered he was more in love with her than ever! And he told here so! This marriage looked like it would be more successful than his first!

For the next few years the marriage looked like a happy one indeed! The only bad thing was Dusty's 1960 miscarriage. All the while Jeff did more films (including a 1958 political one called The Last Hurrah (also directed by John Ford, see above) with the legendary Spencer Tracy, whom Jeff used to watch admiringly on film when he was a boy—see above).

Around 1960 Jeff did another film for Ford (this one was called Sgt. Rutledge). It was about an African-American Sgt. in the 19th century US Army. Jeff played a fellow officer! This film was another well-remembered one (though less so than The Searchers).And it sealed Jeff's western image up even further! Also, in the early 1960's Dusty gave birth to their children together—Henry Herbert McKinnies the Third and his brother Scott! Jeff's family was growing!

In the early 1960's Jeff got one of the greatest roles in his (or any actor's!) entire career! He played Jesus Christ in director Nicholas Ray's remake version of the 1927 religious film King of Kings! Ray (best known for previously directing James Dean in a film and who directed Jeff in True Story of Jesse James—see above) would be directing a religious film of the same name!

There was a January 1961 Modern Screen magazine article by Rev. James H. Kepler (who was a minister of the Church of Our Savior Congregational, Los Angeles, California) that discussed Jeff's part as Jesus in the film. Kepler's article was called "Dare I, a sinner, play Christ?. (J. Kepler had previously been Charlton Heston's spiritual advisor when the latter played Moses in the DeMille-directed 1956 classic The Ten Commandments and comparisons between the performances of the two actors were made in the article.)

Kepler stated that he was sure Hunter had had many sleepless nights as the actor wrestled with his conscience before he decided whether or not to play the Son of God. There was mention of the criticism of the idea of an actor who was divorced in real life playing the sin-free Christ. Kepler wrote that he felt that any actor was just as worthy of playing Christ as any other actor because all people are tainted with original sin.

The article went to also explain how the film was made. Jeff, Dusty and her son Steele all took an apartment in Madrid, Spain during the filming. The lad went to a country day school.

When the scene of the Sermon on the Mount was filmed it was done in a remote region outside of Madrid! The local regional peasants were hired to play the multitude of

Christ worshippers. The film's assistant director announced, in a loud speaker, to the peasants that an actor costumed as Christ was going to be coming among them and to remember that no matter how impressively costumed the actor was he was still only a performer! Jeff started on cue to walk among the Spanish peasants but the sight of him looking and acting so perfectly Christ-like was too much for many of them and they knelt before him actually crossing themselves!

The article had an explanation from Dusty that after Jeff was done portraying the Son of God for the day he was still so in character that it took him three hours to get back to being just Jeffrey Hunter again. (Kepler claimed that in a similar way Heston had lived the part of Moses while playing him!) Also, Jeff would do nothing inconsistent with the part of Christ while dressed as him (Heston wouldn't drink coffee or talk on a telephone while playing Moses). Jeff dedicated himself for the five months he played Jesus to the character. He trusted himself completely to director Nicholas Ray and the spiritual advisors on the film set! He would usually never grant interviews or discuss any of his personal life. Because he wouldn't usually grant interviews the Hollywood press attacked him by claiming how bad it was that a Hollywood cowboy (who was also divorced) got to play the Son of God!

After the filming for KOK wrapped Jeff got a role in one the biggest films he was ever to star in (though his part was small). He played an enlisted man in Darryl F. Zanuck's production of The Longest Day. This film concerned the D-Day Invasion of Normandy in 1944. It had an all star cast which included Richard Burton, Henry Fonda, Paul Anka, again Bob Wagner (Jeff's good friend—see above),Peter Lawford and more. Superstar John Wayne was also in the cast making it Jeff's second film with the Duke (see above)!

More movie work and much more TV work followed The Longest Day for Jeff. He did one ep of The Alfred Hitchcock Hour where he was reunited with his The Searchers co-star comely actress Vera Miles. Jeff played her professor-boyfriend who goes crazy and horribly tries to stab her to death but the beautiful lady is saved by another. The ep ends with Jeff going into a lunatic asylum!

Eventually Jeff and producer/actor Jack Webb (of TV's Dragnet) got professionally together and formed Apollo Productions. This production company of theirs produced a western TV series. It was called Temple Houston and it ran on NBC in the fall of 1963. It starred Jeff as the title character. He played the lawyer-son of Texas president Sam Houston. The production for TH was forced to come up with storyline pretty quick, Jeff later said. He also said that the show was uneven the way it was very serious for the first half of its one season run then became so tongue-in-cheek for it's second half of a season.

Nonetheless, the cancellation of Temple Houston allowed Jeff free to take the role that (along with that of Jesus) became Jeff's other career defining part. It was a role TV star Lloyd Bridges was first offered but rejected. Jeff was cast as Captain Christopher Pike of the starship Enterprise in the Desilu pilot Star Trek*!

*Desilu was a studio which neighbored Paramount Studios at that time. It produced legendary shows like I Love Lucy, The Andy Griffith Show, and The Untouchables.

Gene Roddenberry was producing the pilot. Rodenberry had conceived of the show as a sort of Wagon Train to the Stars. Filming began and ended in December of 1964. A summary of the plot went as follows:

The Space Vehicle Enterprise comes into the orbit of Planet Talos 4. The ship is searching for survivors of the ship The SS Columbia which crashed in the area 18 years before. Beaming down by transporter to the planet's surface Captain Pike, Mr. Spock (Leonard Nimoy) and other Enterprise find what they think is the party of crashed survivors (one of them a very beautiful woman called Vina (Susan Oliver) but it is a trap! The crashed survivors are all an illusion put out by the telepathic Talosian natives of the planet. They kidnap Pike and take him to a cage underground where they subject him to a series of illusions. In most of the illusions Vina returns to him. Pike eventually learns that Vina was a real crashed survivor from the SS Columbia (but, he'll later learn that she is really older and much more disfigured than she usually appears to him) and that the Talosians have been living underground for thousands of centuries since a devastating war on the planet's surface. While underground the Talosians developed great mental powers but they learned it was a trap because they gave up living their own lives pretty much and concentrated too much on illusion. Enterprise Female First Officer Number One (Majel Barrett) and a crewwoman (Laurel Goodwin) beam down and meet up with Pike. With their help the three Enterprise crew members show the Talosians that the former are unsuitable for captivity (as the Enterprise crew prefers death to captivity) and the Talosians release Pike and company as too dangerous a species for Talosian needs. Before going back to the Enterprise Pike learns that Vina is actually badly disfigured and wishes to stay on Talos in the illusion of health and beauty the Talosians constantly give her! Pike and the Enterprise pull out of Talos 4's orbit and head off to their next adventure!

The completed pilot was shown to network executives but, though they liked it a lot, they rejected it as too cerebral for most TV viewers! But in a rare move Roddenberry got the green light to go ahead and make a second pilot. Now different accounts of what happened next start to come into play. One account said that Dusty meddled into her husband's affairs and did so much so that Roddenberry dropped Jeff from the possibility of playing Pike a second time. Another account said the network decided not to use Jeff again. Still other account Jeff did not want to be tied down to playing Pike in a weekly series because it would demand so much of his time. Nevertheless, whatever actually happened Jeff was not in the second pilot (called Where No Man Has Gone Before and of course with William Shatner as Captain James Kirk).

After this Jeff would do more movies and TV work (including guest shots on TV shows like The FBI!). But in early 1967 Dusty announced she was divorcing him. She cited heavy drinking on Jeff's part as a reason! His son, Christopher, much later stated on cable channel E that his father was indeed heavily drinking at this time. And so for a second time Jeff found himself out of a wife and offspring! And BTW this divorce left him rather financially broke too!

Jeff did more acting (including a comedy film with Bob Hope—see Chapter 2). And in January of 1969, now somewhat shaggy haired (it was the late 60's!), he met a new lady in his life. Actress Emily McLaughlin. He met the soap opera actress (from the serial General Hospital) at a party. And romance blossomed quick. Like Jeff, Emily was divorced and had a son from that previous marriage (her son was named Robert).* Interestingly Emily played a nurse on General Hospital and took the part somewhat to heart in real life too!

In February of 1969 the two married in Ciudad Juarez, Chihuahua, Mexico. Jeff's parents gave him a new car as a wedding present. It looked like the start of a good third marriage for Jeff! But fate had other plans.

*Trekkies may want to note that Emily had previously been married to actor Robert Lansing whom she had her son by. Lansing had played Gary Seven in the Star Trek ep Assignment: Earth. This ep was also a pilot for a TV show that never sold!

One night Jeff and Emily were having a turkey dinner and Jeff spilled hot gravy on his pants. He didn't complain but he got rather badly burned from the hot gravy. (Later he had to finally see a doctor about it!) Next the couple went to Spain to film what was to become Jeff's final film (see chapter 2). In one scene a window exploded the wrong way and hit Jeff giving him a concussion! He recovered and later a friend of his fooled around with Jeff and gave him a karate chop which Jeff right into a door and he banged his already injured head! The film producers were running out of money and they couldn't pay most of the cast playing in the film with Jeff so Jeff himself decided to end work on the film and go back to the US with Emily! On the plane he got semi-paralyzed in his arm and became incapable of much speech! As soon as the plane landed in California he was rushed to the hospital (fittingly called The Good Samaritan) by ambulance and they found little wrong with him! Some vertebra was out of place. They weren't sure which of Jeff's accidents caused this. He stayed in the hospital a couple of days (and he watched his new wife on General Hospital while he was there!).

As soon as he was released and well enough Jeff bought Emily a very nice ring for their marriage (he had only purchased a small one in Mexico when they married).

All was starting to look good again. Jeff was even signed to star in a project with Vince Edwards (of TV's Ben Casey) called A Band of Brothers. Jeff was also trying to get to star with Emily on General Hospital. Then in May 26, 1969 Emily went to work at the TV studio and she left work having a funny feeling about things. She drove home to their house in Van Nuys and found Jeff unconscious on the stairs! He had fallen down! An ambulance was called quickly (a news source of the tragic incident at the time said a friend of Jeff's called the fire department for the ambulance—Emily would later recollect that she made the call)! Jeff was rushed to the Valley Receiving Hospital. While he was in the hospital Emily's ex-husband Robert came to comfort her (but she was probably under sedation while Robert stood over her)! After a long operation to save Jeff's life he was pronounced dead the next morning! A Van Nuys policeman, Detective Sgt. Jesse A. Tubbs was called in to investigate---- Jeff's death was found to be an accident! From a fall on the stairs though one of his eyes was swollen and he likely had fallen after losing the ability to stay conscious due to his previous head injuries! Hollywood was out a talented and popular performer, several boys were out a caring father and his last wife was left with so little reason to live she almost died very soon after the incident (she just managed to in fact survive until the 1990's)!

The still young actor very quickly had his funeral mass held at the St. Mark's Episcopal Church in Van Nuys, California. He was buried in Glenhaven Cemetery in San Fernando, California.

A last word. Nobody knows what Jeffrey Hunter's life would have been like had he survived into the 1970's and beyond. My own personal guess is that he would have made more film dramas (maybe even a strong supporting role in a Clint Eastwood Dirty Harry film) and demonstrated the ability to show off an even deeper style of acting than the 50's and 60's films gave him. Whatever would have became of Jeff had he lived is, again, guesswork but we do have plenty of fine film and TV work to watch and admire from the acting legacy that was Jeffrey Hunter!

Chapter 2

Jeffrey Hunter's filmography and some film reviews

What Film Critics Said of Jeffrey Hunter's work

Dreamboat (1952)

(This film concerned a veteran film actor-turned Professor with a young daughter—the daughter was played by comely Anne Francis---Jeff played the daughter's escort!)
In his July 26, 1952 film review New York Times critic Bosley Crowther said Hunter and Francis were pleasant in their romantic, young stuff.

The Searchers (1956)

In his May 31, 1956 NY Times review Bosley Crowther claimed Hunter is wonderfully callow and courageous as the lad who goes along with John Wayne's uncommonly commanding and vengeful Texan character.

Sergeant Rutledge (1960)

The May 26, 1960 NY Times review of this John Ford-directed film says that Hunter was rather persuasive as a man befriending the title character.

King of Kings (1961)

In his October 12, 1961 NY Times film review of KOK Bosley Crowther wrote of Hunter that the actor wore his Christ makeup nobly and performed his part with taste and simplicity.

The Longest Day (1962)

Bosley Crowther's October 5, 1962 NY Times film review of this classic did not single out Hunter's performance (outside of mentioning in a cast list that Jeff played Sgt. Fuller).
My take on this part: Hunter is natural and very convincing playing the romantically troubled enlisted man who (true to the nature of making fast mutual friends in war) spills his beans (about a girl) to a fellow serviceman who is in fact a stranger to him. Hunter has an effective death scene too!

Brainstorm (1965)

A June 10, 1965 article New York Times article reviewing this film said that Jeffrey Hunter was a fine young actor who is hopelessly miscast in the part of an individual who is cunning and diabolical. That Hunter looked too intelligent and also decent for the character.

(This film reunited Jeff with his Dreamboat co-star Anne Francis!)

The Private Navy of Sgt. O'Farrell

In her May 9, 1968 review of this film (also starring the Bob Hope and Phyllis Diller)
Renata Adler simply mentioned Jeff in the cast list, but gave no review of his work!
My own thoughts on Jeff's performance. He has some great moments playing it straight
(but not overly serious) opposite Diller!

Selected Filmography

1) Julius Caesar (1949)
Director: David Bradley
Some other cast members: Charlton Heston, Harold Tasker

2) Call Me Mister (1951)
Directed by Lloyd Bacon
Some other cast members: Betty Grable, Dan Daily

3) Fourteen Hours (1951)
Directed by Henry Hathaway
Some other cast members: Paul Douglas, Richard Basehart

4) The Frogmen (1951)
Director: Lloyd Bacon
Some other cast members: Richard Widmark, Dana Andrews

5) Take of My Little Girl (1951)
Director: Jean Negulesco
Some other cast members: Jeanne Crain, Mitzi Gaynor

6) Red Skies of Montana (1951)
Director: Joseph Newman
Some other cast members: Richard Widmark, Constance Smith

7) Belles on their Toes (1952)
Director: Henry Levin
Some other cast members: Jeanne Crain, Myrna Loy

8) Lure of the Wilderness (1952)
Director: Jean Negulesco
Some other cast members: Jean Peters, Walter Brennan

9) Dreamboat (1952)
Director: Claude Binyon
Some other cast members: Ginger Rogers, Anne Francis

10) Single Handed (1953)
Director: Harmon Jones
Some other cast members: Michael Rennie, Debra Paget

11) Seven Angry Men (1955)
Director: Charles Marquis Warren
Some other cast members: Raymond Massey, Debra Paget

12) The Searchers (1956)
Director: John Ford
Some other cast members: John Wayne, Natalie Wood

13) True Story of Jesse James (1957)
Director: Nicholas Ray
Some other cast members: Robert Wagner, Hope Lange

14) The Last Hurrah (1958)
Director: John Ford
Some other cast members: Spencer Tracy, Pat O'Brien

15) King of Kings (1961)
Director: Nicholas Ray
Some other cast members: Robert Ryan, Hurd Hatfield

16) The Longest Day (1962)
Directors: Ken Annakin, Andrew Marton, Bernhard Wicki, (Darryl F. Zanuck—uncredited)
Some others cast members: John Wayne, Robert Mitchum

17) Brainstorm (1965)
Director: William Conrad
Some other cast members: Anne Francis, Kathie Browne

18) The Private Navy of Sgt. O'Farrell (1968)
Director: Frank Tashlin
Some other cast members: Bob Hope, Phyllis Diller

19) Viva America
Director: Javier Seto
Some other cast members: Margaret Lee, Pier Angeli
(Hunter's last film-- released after his death!)

Bibliography:

1) www.imdb.com--Their article on Jeffrey Hunter

2) www.jeffreyhuntermovies.com/newsite/inprint.htm

3) "Up Till Now: The Autobiography" by William Shatner and David Fisher; Thomas Dunne Books, 2008

Also by Michelle Bernier

"Charlton Heston: An Incredible Life: Revised Edition" Createspace, 2009